STOCK MARKET abc

Illustrated by
Tom Dunnington

STOCK MARKET abc

Joanne K. Friedlander
and Jean Neal

Follett Publishing Company
Chicago New York

The authors gratefully acknowledge stock brokers Gerald Fleischman, of Goodbody & Company, and Herbert H. Lipson, of Rodman and Renshaw, for their assistance in preparing this book.

 Manufactured in the United States of America. Published simultaneously in Canada by The Ryerson Press, Toronto.

SBN 695-48356-0 Titan binding
SBN 695-88356-9 Trade binding

Library of Congress Catalog Card Number: 69-15097

First Printing

FOR OUR CHILDREN

MARK, SUE, GRIFF, AND LESLIE ELIZABETH

Contents

STOCK MARKET abc

FERTILIZER

1
How To Make Money Grow

Blue chips continue to gain.
Wall Street had its busiest day today.
The Dow-Jones Averages showed an increase.
Standard Oil is up two points.
The stock market closed higher today.

How strange, yet familiar, these phrases are. We see them in newspapers and hear them on radio and television. They seem to belong to a mysterious world, the world of business and finance, a world that makes money grow.

Although this world seems strange and complicated, anyone, even a child, can be a part of it. The passport is to become an investor. Investors are people who put aside money now that will make more money in the future. Anyone who wants to make his savings earn more money can become an investor.

Suppose a beginning investor has saved or received a gift of $200, which he wants to keep for the future. If he put that $200 in a piggy bank, ten years from now he would have exactly what he put in the bank—$200. But ten years from now, with prices constantly going up, that $200 will probably buy much less than it does today. A motorbike that costs $200 now might cost $300 then. This pattern of continually rising prices is called inflation.

Our beginning investor, of course, does not want his $200 to be worth less in the future than it is now. So, to combat the increase in prices, he must find a way to increase the value of his money. The only way to do this is through wise investment.

One form of investment is a savings account at the bank. There the investor's money will earn a certain amount of additional money, called interest. This is what the bank pays the investor for the use of his money. If put in the bank, the money would stand little risk of being lost and would always be available if needed.

Important as it is to have a savings account at a bank, this by itself may not be our investor's best investment for the future. Because by law a bank can pay only a set amount of interest on savings, the value of the investor's money may not grow fast enough to keep up with rising prices.

To increase his savings sufficiently for the future, he may need another form of investment—the stock market. He can invest in the stock market by buying a share, or part ownership, of a business. Buying a share of a company is the same as buying stock in it. By owning stock in a good company, a person's investment should grow as that company grows.

Money invested in the stock market can grow more than money put in the bank. There are two reasons for this. First is higher growth. If our beginning investor uses his $200 to buy stock in a growing company, he may in time be able to sell his stock for much more than the $200 he paid for it. Unlike interest on savings, there is no set limit to profit on stocks. Second is dividends. During the years the investor owns a company's stock, he will probably receive a part of the company's profits, called dividends. Thus, as the company grows more prosperous, so do the people who own stock in it.

Sometimes a person can be very lucky in choosing which stock to buy, and when to buy it. For example, suppose a man named Mr. Adams bought stock in Chrysler Corporation, the maker of Chrysler automobiles, in 1958. At that time it cost Mr.

Adams $200 to buy 18 shares of Chrysler stock. Ten years later, the price of Chrysler stock had risen so high that Mr. Adams sold his shares for about $2,200. Not only did he make a profit of $2,000 from his $200 investment, but during those ten years he also received a yearly dividend from the company.

Most people are not fortunate enough to make such a profit. Mr. Adams happened to invest in the stock market at a time when stock prices were low and were rising very rapidly, and he was fortunate to choose a stock that climbed so high in price.

Despite the good fortune of people like Mr. Adams, all investors must remember that buying shares of stock in a company has its risks as well as its rewards. Stock prices can fall as well as rise. At worst, a company could run into serious trouble and an investor could lose all the money he paid for its shares.

Because there is a risk in buying stock, no one should do so unless he first has a savings account at a bank. That money will always be on hand for emergencies. Money invested in the stock market should be money set aside after savings.

BOND
STOCK
DIVIDEND

2

Stocks, Bonds, and Dividends

The stock market is made up of some of America's biggest, most important companies—and the people who own them. These companies cover every industry. They include railroads and airlines; the companies that supply gas, electricity, and telephones; the manufacturing firms that produce cars, furniture, food, and nearly everything else we use; and the businesses that sell these things.

Because they hold, or own, shares of stock in these companies, the company owners are known as stockholders. Stockholders are people of all kinds—men, women, and children of every race, creed, and occupation.

A company that sells shares of itself is called a corporation. A corporation sells shares because it often needs money. It may need money to buy new machinery or to build more factories or to hire more workers.

For example, World Wide Toy Company may want to expand and make golf clubs as well as toys. It believes it can manufacture a better golf club that will be more popular than any now on the market. The company's management is convinced it can increase its profits by supplying these clubs. Because its factories are set up only for toy making, World Wide must build new factories and equip them with the machinery to make golf clubs. To get money for this, it may decide to sell shares of itself. These shares are called securities, which is another name for stocks and bonds.

As explained earlier, stocks are the same things as shares. When an investor buys stock in a company, he buys a share of that company and becomes a part owner of it. The extent of his ownership depends upon the number of shares available in the company and the number of shares he owns. General Motors, for example, has 285,583,000 shares of stock outstanding, or owned by stockholders. Therefore, a stockholder who owns 10 shares of General Motors stock owns $^{10}/_{285,583,000}$ of the company's factories, laboratories, equipment, and everything else that is part of the company.

There are two kinds of stock—preferred and common.

Preferred stock earns for its holders a certain amount of money, paid at regular times each year. This money is called a fixed dividend. If a company pays a dividend, or a share of its profits, to its stockholders, holders of preferred stock always receive their money first, before a cent is paid to the common stockholders. This is why it is called "preferred."

Why doesn't everyone want to buy preferred stock, then? The answer is that although preferred stockholders are sure of getting their share of the company's profits, their share is a limited amount only. This is not true of common stock.

The dividend paid on common stock is not fixed, or limited. Nor is it guaranteed. Therefore, holders of common stock take a bigger risk of not being paid for their investment. In return for this risk, though, they often receive a greater share of a company's profits than preferred stockholders. That is why common stock can grow and make more money in the long run.

Because of this potential for growth, more people buy common stock than preferred. Besides, it is usually much less expensive. Preferred stock is bought mainly by insurance companies and other investment groups.

PREFERRED
COMMON

Bonds are entirely different from stocks. When an investor buys a company's bond, he is lending that company his money. In return for the loan, the company pays him interest, or a set price for the use of his money, just as a bank pays interest on a savings account. For instance, if a person owns a government savings bond, he is loaning his money to the government, and the government pays him interest for the use of that money.

If a company needs money for a specific length of time, it may issue bonds. If it doesn't want a debt that must be paid back at a certain time, it may decide to raise money by issuing stock instead of bonds. Many companies do both. Because bonds are rarely sold for less than $1,000, they are not of much interest to the beginning investor.

Dividends, however, are of interest to all investors.

Every company wants investors to want its stock. Therefore, when a company is making money, it usually gives its stockholders a dividend, or a share of its profits. The company's officers—its board of directors—decide whether or not the company should pay a dividend.

Sometimes these men may decide that profits must go into research or building more factories, instead of into the stockholders' pockets. Usually, though, a successful company pays its stockholders at regular times each year, every three or six months.

To see how dividends are paid, suppose an investor bought 100 shares of Midwest Airlines for $20 a share, and the directors of Midwest declare a dividend of $1 a share. Because he owns 100 shares, the investor would receive $100 a year in dividends.

Besides money dividends, companies can also declare stock dividends. This means they give the stockholders more shares of their stock, rather than money. A company may have had a very prosperous year, but its directors may want to hold on to its profits for research or new equipment. They may decide it would not be wise to spend any money in dividends at this time. So the company declares a stock dividend instead of a money dividend.

Let's say that the directors of Midwest Airlines decide to give each stockholder a dividend of two shares for every 100 shares he already owns. A stockholder who owns 100 shares would then own 102 shares. If this person needs money, he can sell his stock dividend and still own as many shares as before.

Although not a dividend, stock splits are another way in which companies can change the number of shares owned by stockholders. When a company declares a stock split, it gives each stockholder a certain number of shares for every share he already owns. Usually a stock split is 2-for-1 or 3-for-1—that is, two or three shares for every share already owned.

Although a stock split may double or triple the number of shares owned by a stockholder, it does not double or triple the present value of his investment in the company. The reason for this is that with every stock split, there is a reduction in stock price. On a 2-for-1 split, the price of each share is cut approximately in half. On a 3-for-1 split, each share becomes worth about a third of its previous price. In this way a stock split changes the number of shares owned by a stockholder and the price of each share, but it does not change the total value of his investment. That remains the same.

A typical stock split would work like this. An investor owns 100 shares of Midwest Airlines priced at $20 a share, for a total investment of $2,000. The directors of Midwest announce a 2-for-1 stock split. The investor would then get two shares for every one he owns, or a total of 200 shares. However, the price of each share would be cut in half to $10. Two hundred shares priced at $10 a share

HOW A STOCK SPLIT WORKS

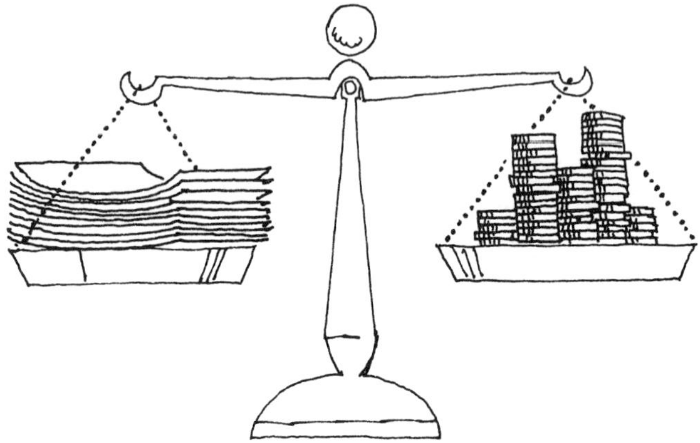

Before split, investor owns 100 shares of stock priced at $20 a share. His total investment is $2,000.

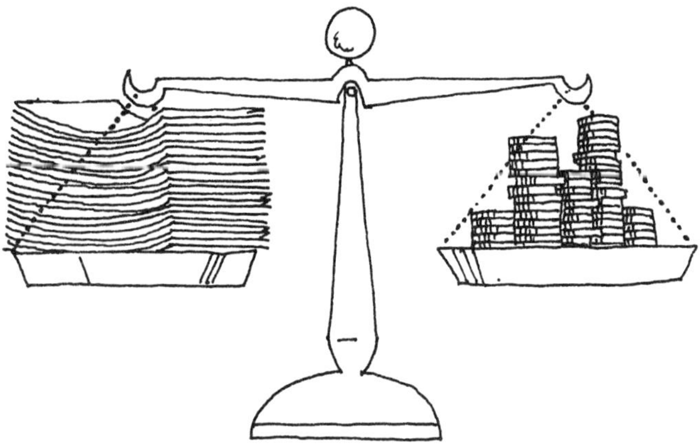

After 2-for-1 split, investor owns twice as many shares at half the original price, or 200 shares at $10 a share. His total investment is still $2,000.

gives the stockholder a total investment of $2,000—the same as he had before. Only the number of shares he owns and the price per share have changed.

Companies declare stock splits mainly to obtain more money. A split lowers the price of a stock so more people can afford to buy it. As more people buy, the company gets more money. Also, the stock is kept active and in circulation.

A stock split often benefits stockholders, too. It stirs people's interest in the stock, and as more people want to buy it, its price rises, giving the stockholders a higher profit if and when they sell it.

STOCK MARKET
WELCOME
GUIDE
BROKER

3
Entering the Stock Market

Once a beginning investor has decided to buy stock, he needs to know where to go and whom to see. This is the time for his first visit to a stock broker. If his hometown is so small there is no broker, the local banker will offer the same sort of service.

Every major city in the United States has brokerage firms where stock brokers work. Brokers are experts in stock trading, the business of buying and selling securities. A broker's job is bringing together people who want to buy stocks and people who want to sell them. His value to buyers and sellers is his training and his up-to-date knowledge of what's going on in the stock market.

To become a broker, a man must have passed a rigid examination covering every phase of the investment market. His day to day activities—the businessmen he knows and the publications he reads—keep him well informed about the financial world.

That's why a beginning investor should seek and respect his advice.

From city to city brokerage offices are very much alike. A broker, or customer's man, will be happy to show a first-time visitor around the firm.

The large room usually entered first is called the boardroom. It is open to the public during trading hours (10 a.m. to 3:30 p.m. Eastern Standard Time). On one wall of the boardroom a stock market ticker tape is projected and magnified, somewhat like a movie. A ticker tape is a cellophane ribbon on which an electric machine prints stock transactions. A stock transaction occurs whenever shares are bought or sold. The ticker tape sends information on stock transactions from one place to another much like the telegraph.

On the tape each stock has its own symbol, which may or may not hint at the name of the company. For example, GM is General Motors; X is United States Steel. Learning to read the tape means memorizing the symbols for company names.

Each stock symbol, as it appears on the ticker tape, is followed by the number of shares that were traded (in units of 100) and the price at which it was sold. If the price immediately follows the symbol, this means 100 shares were traded. For ex-

CFD
3s24 1/4
PCG
36s. 10.100
FWPr
2

ample, GE85½ means 100 shares of General Electric were sold for $85.50 per share. RCA5s47¼ means 500 shares of Radio Corporation of America sold for $47.25 a share. If a trade involves 1,000 shares or more, the full number is written out on the tape, like this: GM1.000s80, which means 1,000 shares of General Motors sold for $80 a share. On the tape periods replace commas in large numbers.

On the ticker tape and elsewhere in the business world, stock prices are not given in terms of dollars. Instead, they are given as points. Points mean dollars. If a business report says a stock is up 2 points, it means that the stock has risen $2 in price. Fractions of points are parts of a dollar. All fractions of stock prices are given in units of ⅛. This means that ⅛ is 12½¢, ¼ is 25¢, ⅝ is 62½¢, and so on up to $1.

Besides the ticker tape, the boardroom of a brokerage firm usually contains wire and teletype equipment. This equipment is connected with the firm's New York office and with the New York Stock Exchange, where most stock transactions are actually made.

When an investor decides to buy or sell a stock, his broker phones or teletypes the order to his firm's office in New York City. From there it is relayed

their products or service, and for their ability to pay dividends in good times and bad. Usually these stocks are relatively high priced. Their dividends are regular, but seldom spectacular. One remarkably dependable blue-chip company is Penn Central, which operates a major railroad; it has paid a dividend every year for over 120 years.

2. Growth—Shares in companies in new or growing industries, like transistors or plastics, which over a period of time seem sure to expand greatly. These young companies often must skip dividends to build new plants or to invest heavily in research and development. Their ultimate growth is the attraction.

3. Income Growth—Shares in companies in well-established, essential industries, like public transportation and food processing, which are still growing. Their stocks pay regular dividends and, in time, can increase in value considerably. Income-growth stocks are popular because they offer a fairly safe way for investors to take a small risk in return for some future growth potential.

4. Cyclical—Shares in industries that are affected quickly and drastically by the overall business condition of the country. Cyclical stocks include some of the biggest firms in America. For example,

TREET JOURNAL
BROKER
GROWTH
BLUE CHIPS
CYCLICAL

General Motors and United States Steel are cyclical stocks because a mild business rise or decline can quickly cause a speedup or a slowdown in orders for products like automobiles or farm machinery. Because of how suddenly such industries are affected, the prices of stocks in these companies change rapidly. Therefore, they offer the greatest risk. But if invested in at the right time, they sometimes offer the greatest rewards. Because of their perilous nature, high-risk, high-reward stocks are often called speculative.

As an investor matures and becomes more familiar with the stock market—and often as his earnings increase—he will buy stocks in various industries. This is called diversification. By spreading his investments among different kinds of companies, he hopes to protect his money. Then, if one industry is hit by bad times and falling stock prices, he still has his investments in other industries to balance the loss.

When an investor refers to his stock portfolio, he already has diversified his investments. A portfolio means all the securities an investor owns. It may include bonds and preferred shares as well as common stocks.

Once a beginner understands the kinds of investments he can make in common stocks, there are several ways that a broker can help him make a wise decision. One important way is by providing information.

Every corporation that sells shares of stock publishes a financial statement once a year. This is called an annual report, and it is available from any brokerage firm. This report tells how much money the company is earning, how much money it owes, and how much profit it made during the previous year.

A company's annual report, though often difficult reading, can also provide more than statistics on profit and loss. For instance, an annual report often tells how and where a company has diversified (how many different businesses it has an interest in), its plans for expansion, its dividend policy, its management-labor relationships, and other company conditions. This is typical of the kind of information a broker is also able to provide through the reports of his own office's research department and the technical publications he reads.

Suppose a young investor has returned from his broker's office with several booklets and reports on growth companies. He has discussed his investment plan with his parents, and they agree with the

broker's recommendation that he should buy stock in a company with good prospects for future expansion.

Among the companies he studies, one name is already familiar to him—Super Wheels, Inc. He has a bike and a motor scooter equipped with wheels made by the company. As he studies the information provided by his broker, he learns that Super Wheels is expanding into different fields and plans to export some of its products the following year. The company's management has been highly recommended by the broker, and its common stock is already paying $1 yearly dividend. Both the young investor and his parents believe that Super Wheels is a wise choice for his first stock purchase.

At this point they could simply telephone the broker and ask him to place an order for the stock. But, since this is a first stock purchase, they decide to return to the broker's office to complete the transaction.

This is how it is done. The broker first gets a quote, which is the current trading price, on Super Wheels. To do this, he uses an electronic device that is connected directly to the New York Stock Exchange. In a few seconds he reports the stock is "19½ to 19¾." This means that $19.50 is the highest price any buyer wants to pay and that $19.75 is the lowest price any seller will take at the time the quote was given on the floor of the exchange. Super Wheels, then, is selling for about $20 a share. With his $200, the young investor can afford 10 shares of stock.

Because the law says no one under 21 may own stock in his own name, the purchase is made in his parents' name. The broker teletypes his New York office to purchase 10 shares of Super Wheels "at the market." This means at the best price available when the order actually reaches the floor of the exchange.

The teletype message is received by a clerk in the order department of the New York office. He telephones it to a member of the firm working on the floor of the stock exchange. By the time the order reaches this man, the price of Super Wheels may be a fraction higher or lower than the one quoted by the broker because of the speed at which prices change during trading.

At this moment, as his order is being processed on the floor of the stock exchange, the investor has truly entered the stock market, heart of America's financial world.

NEW YORK STOCK EXCHANGE

4
The New York Stock Exchange

The New York Stock Exchange is about as old as the United States. It was organized shortly after the Revolutionary War.

At that time the nation was growing rapidly, and more and more people were settling in cities. Because these people could no longer grow their own food or make many other things they needed, factories and businesses were started. Owners needed money to build their plants and stores and to buy raw materials and supplies. The banks did not have enough money to loan to all of the businessmen, so some of these men incorporated their businesses and sold stock in them.

At the same time Congress authorized an issue of $80 million in government stock to help pay the costs of the Revolutionary War. But people were reluctant to invest their money in either business or the government, for they had no assurance they could sell their securities when they wanted to.

In 1792 a group of 24 merchants and auctioneers met under a buttonwood tree on Wall Street in New York City. Their aim was to help new businesses and the government raise money. They decided to meet under the tree at regular hours each day to buy and sell securities. This would give people a marketplace where they could buy and sell their stock whenever they wished. These 24 men were the original members of the New York Stock Exchange.

A year later the men moved into the Tontine Coffee House, a nearby restaurant. There the growing business of stock trading continued.

In the peaceful times after the War of 1812, new businesses developed and established businesses expanded. Soon the stock brokers outgrew the coffee house and moved to a new meeting room on Wall Street. Greater activity brought the need for a more formal set of rules and regulations, and in 1817 the first constitution of the New York Stock Exchange Board was adopted. After that the exchange moved many times to different quarters before settling, in 1863, upon the site of the present building.

Today visitors to New York City find the big,

ye old
Wall Street
FRANKLIN
KITE
ACME
BUGGY WHIP

bustling financial district, called Wall Street, a landmark to remember. Here, at the corner of Broad and Wall streets, stands the large building known as the New York Stock Exchange. This is the place where companies sell their stock and where brokers buy and sell stock for their customers.

An elevator carries visitors to a gallery two stories above the trading floor. A uniformed guide explains the activity below to the people.

The trading floor is about as large as a football field. It is one of the busiest, noisiest places in the world. From 10 a.m., when the trading day opens, until 3:30 p.m., when it ends, there may be as many as 18 million shares of stock traded.

The floor is divided into three rooms. Scattered about the rooms are nineteen horseshoe-shaped trading centers, called posts. Each post has about 75 stocks assigned to it.

Along the sides of the floor clerks at telephones and teletype machines take orders to buy and sell. Above the floor a ticker tape is projected on giant screens. This ticker tape keeps the men on the floor informed of the sales going on all around them.

On two other walls are large boards on which numbers are flashed. These numbers call the men on the floor who are trading. If a broker's number appears on the board, he knows he has a phone call or other message.

The men on the floor are members of the exchange. To be a member of the New York Stock Exchange, a man must own a membership, or seat, as it is usually called. Membership in the exchange is worth a great deal of money because only a limited number are available. Today the cost of buying a seat from a member who is willing to sell his seat is about $250,000. The price, however, has varied over the years from $17,000 in 1942 to a high of $625,000 in 1928 and 1929.

There are 1,366 members of the exchange, and the firms to which these members belong are known as member firms. Only members are permitted to do business on the floor of the exchange.

About half the members belong to firms that do business for the public. These men are the commission brokers who represent the investor.

Besides the brokers handling orders for their customers, there are about 350 men called specialists and dealers on the trading floor.

The specialist is always standing at the post where his assigned stocks are traded. It is his job to handle orders to buy and sell these stocks for brokers. It is also his job to buy and sell for his own account to maintain a stable market at all times. For instance, sometimes a broker may come to a trading post with an order to sell a stock and no other broker is there with an order to buy that stock. Then the specialist must step in and bid to buy the stock for his own account.

The specialist is not expected to keep a stock from climbing or falling in price. He is, however, expected to try to keep rises and declines fair and orderly. To do this, he often must risk his own money by buying stock for a price higher than others are willing to pay at that time. He also often has to

sell stock for less than others are willing to sell.

Other members on the trading floor of the exchange are known as floor brokers, or $2 brokers. These men assist the commission brokers when they have too many orders to handle by themselves. A floor broker is really a broker for a broker. The name "$2 broker" is a holdover from the days when the commission they received was $2 for every 100 shares they handled. Today their commission is determined by the price of the stock involved.

Another group of men on the floor act as odd-lot dealers. These men make it possible for an investor to buy one share of stock as easily as 100 shares. For all but a few very expensive stocks, an odd lot is any number of shares from 1 to 99. A round lot is 100 shares. Odd-lot dealers buy round lots of 100 shares and then resell the shares in odd lots to brokers at the current price. When brokers have an order from a customer for less than 100 shares, they buy from, or sell to, an odd-lot dealer.

For his services the odd-lot dealer receives 12½¢ a share on stock selling for less than $40 a share, or 25¢ a share on stock selling for $40 or more a share. This charge is added directly to the price of the stock.

A small group of exchange members are not

brokers, specialists, or odd-lot dealers. They are floor traders, who buy and sell only for themselves. Although floor traders work for their own profit, they perform a service for the market, too. Their buying and selling helps to narrow the range between prices bid and prices asked for stock.

The other people on the floor are paid employees of the exchange. Some are clerks who stand behind the trading post counters to help with orders. Others, called reporters, stand outside each trading post and see that the price indicator on the post is changed after each sale. Circulating around the floor are page boys who send reports of each sale to the ticker room.

As explained earlier, the stock exchange is a marketplace where buyers and sellers of stocks can meet to trade, and where businesses can sell their stock. The exchange works like a two-way auction. Buyers compete with each other to buy at the lowest possible price, while sellers compete to sell at the highest possible price. When a buyer and a seller agree on a price, a sale is made.

The role the stock exchange plays may be explained by these four points:

1. When an investor buys, he buys from another person.

2. When he sells, he sells to another person.

3. The stock exchange itself does not buy, sell, or set prices.

4. The exchange simply provides the marketplace.

To see how a trade is made on the floor of the exchange, let's follow our beginning investor's order to buy 10 shares of Super Wheels. However, let's make it a more typical transaction by pretending the order was for a round lot, or 100 shares, instead.

After the investor placed his order, his broker teletyped it to his New York office, which relayed the call to the trading floor of the New York Stock Exchange. Here the order is received by a clerk in the brokerage firm's booth on the floor. He writes it out in a kind of shorthand and gives it to the firm's commission broker. If the broker is not at the booth, the clerk can call him by pushing a button that flashes the broker's number on the big wall board.

Having received the order, the broker goes to the trading post where Super Wheels is bought and sold. The price indicator on the post says the last sale in Super Wheels was 19¾, or $19.75 a share. Several brokers are at the post, making bids below the price the sellers are asking. The beginning investor's broker decides to make a bid for his client.

"One half for one hundred," he says, which means he'll pay $19.50 a share for 100 shares. If he gets no response, he may raise his bid by ⅛ of a point, or 12½¢. "Five-eighths for one hundred," he says, raising the price to $19.62½ a share.

The broker who offered to sell the stock at 19¾ now decides he can't get that price and accepts the bid of the broker representing the beginning investor. The selling broker simply says, "Sold," nods his head, and the transaction is over. No written agreements are exchanged by the brokers. All bids to buy and offers to sell must be made aloud.

As soon as the trade is completed, the brokers make a record of the transaction, and a report is phoned back to their offices so that each customer can be informed.

At the same time, after the sale, one of the four or five exchange reporters who stand outside each trading post sees that the price indicator on the post is changed from 19¾ to 19⅝. A reporter also writes a report of the sale. He then gives the report to a page boy who takes it to the pneumatic tube leading directly from each post to the ticker room. Immediately the ticker tape shows SW19⅝ not only on the screens above the exchange floor, but on more than 3,300 screens and stock tickers

A TYPICAL STOCK TRANSACTION

THE ASKING PRICE

Super Wheels at 19¾.
($19.75)

THE FIRST BID
BY INVESTOR'S BROKER

One-half for one hundred.
($19.50 for 100 shares)

NO RESPONSE

THE SECOND BID
BY INVESTOR'S BROKER

Five-eighths for one hundred.
($19.62½ for 100 shares)

Sold!

THE NEW ASKING
PRICE AFTER SALE

Super Wheels at 19⅝.
($19.62½)

in cities throughout the United States.

After the market closes for the day, the two brokerage firms involved in the trade arrange for the actual transfer of stock and payment of the amount due. All settlements between member firms are arranged through the New York Stock Exchange Clearing Corporation, so that a minimum of cash and securities is handled.

Now that we have seen how a typical round-lot transaction is handled, let's follow an odd-lot trade. The commission broker on the floor of the exchange has just received the beginning investor's order for 10 shares of Super Wheels. He gives the order to an odd-lot dealer at the Super Wheels trading post. At the moment the dealer receives the order, Super Wheels is selling at 19⅝, or \$19.62½. When the odd-lot dealer fills the order, he bills the broker for 10 shares at 19¾, or \$19.75 a share. This mark-up for his services is the standard ⅛ of a point, or 12½¢, on each share of stock selling for less than \$40 a share.

The beginning investor's order would be only one of thousands transacted during a trading day. As many as 40,000 such sales in one day is not unusual.

The shares of more than 1,400 corporations

may be bought and sold on the New York Stock Exchange. Ten of the most widely owned companies listed on the exchange are: American Telephone and Telegraph, General Motors, Standard Oil of New Jersey, General Electric, General Telephone and Electronics, United States Steel, Ford Motor Company, Bethlehem Steel, E.I. duPont de Nemours, and Socony Mobil Oil.

Not every company may sell its stock on the New York Stock Exchange. To be listed on the exchange, a company must meet certain strict requirements. It must show an earning power of at least 1 million dollars a year and own assets of at least 10 million dollars. It must have at least 1,500 stockholders already, with at least 500,000 shares distributed among them. In addition, the company must be operating successfully, its products must be important, and it must have a good position in its industry.

Another organization concerned with the record of a company is the Securities and Exchange Commission, which was established by Congress to regulate all brokers who handle listed stocks.

Unfortunately, some people have the idea that the commission's approval of stock for public sale means that the stock is a good investment. This is not true. The commission can only try to make sure that the company's reputation is satisfactory, that its stock is fairly offered, and that it will abide by the rules of selling stock as set down in the Securities Exchange Act of 1934. The commission cannot guarantee that the stock will be a profitable investment.

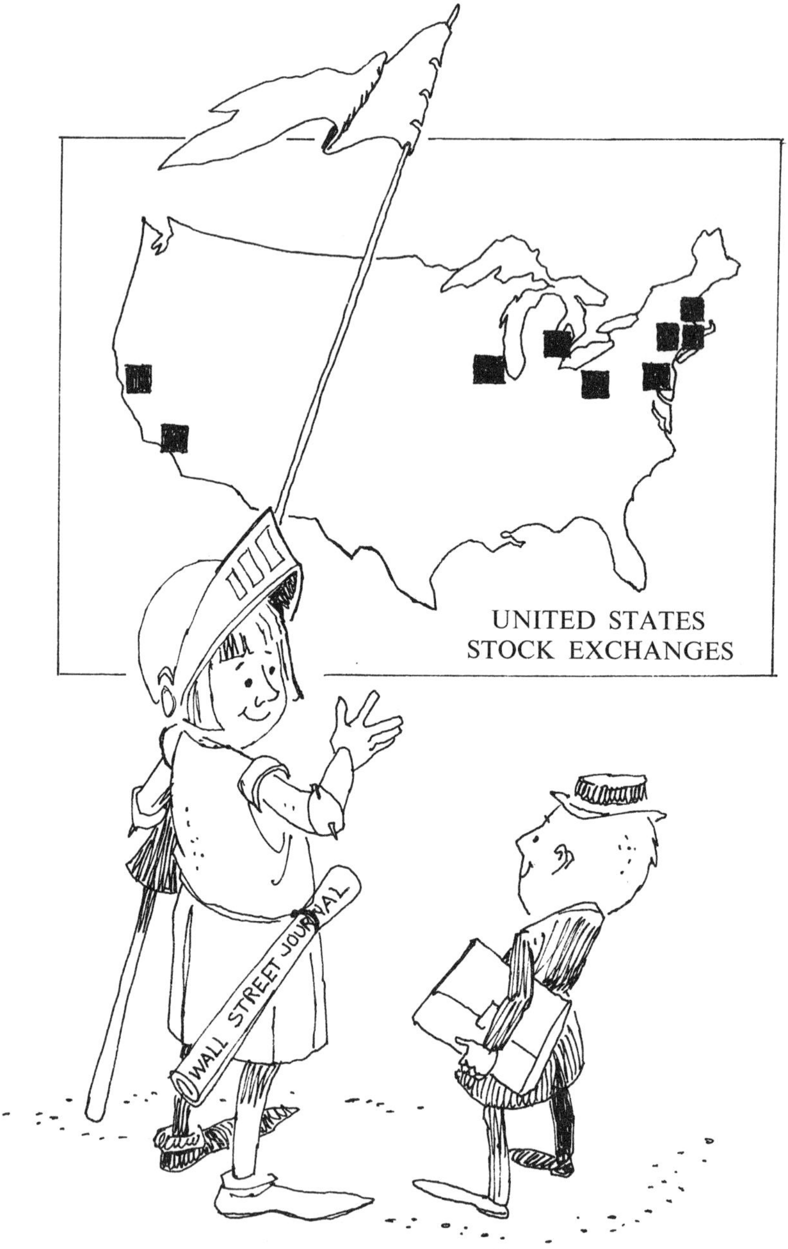
UNITED STATES
STOCK EXCHANGES
WALL STREET JOURNAL

5

Other Exchanges and the Over-the-Counter Market

Although the New York Stock Exchange is by far the largest, it is not the only stock exchange in the United States. The second largest one is the American Stock Exchange, which is also in New York City. More than 1,000 stocks are listed on this exchange.

In addition to those two exchanges, there are six others: the Midwest Exchange in Chicago, the Baltimore-Philadelphia-Washington Exchange in Philadelphia, the Boston Stock Exchange, the Detroit Stock Exchange, the Pittsburgh Stock Exchange, and the West Coast Stock Exchange in Los Angeles and San Francisco. These smaller exchanges usually handle businesses in their own region. Smaller companies find it much easier to list their stock on the regional exchanges than on the two big ones in New York.

Although approximately 3,500 companies are

listed on the major stock exchanges, many more companies sell their stock without benefit of an exchange. Such stocks are sold in the over-the-counter market and are known as OTC's.

When a company first goes public—that is, when it first sells stock in itself—it joins the over-the-counter market. No one knows for sure just how many companies are in the OTC market, but most experts guess there are more than 175,000. These firms range all the way from small bicycle

shops to multimillion-dollar corporations, like the well-known drug firm, Eli Lilly and Co., and the huge magazine publisher, Time Inc. Many local utility companies and nearly all bank and insurance companies are OTC stocks.

Buying and selling in the OTC market is completely different from trading on the New York Stock Exchange. Instead of the auction type bidding practiced on the exchange, the OTC market depends upon negotiated transactions. This means that when

an OTC broker goes to buy a stock for his customer, he must buy the stock at a price that is low enough to provide him with his own profit when he sells it to his customer. The price at which the OTC broker sells a stock, therefore, is determined by the price he must pay to get it, since he does not get a commission.

If an investor wanted to buy 100 shares of Magic Metal, Inc., an over-the-counter stock, he would call his local OTC broker and give him the order. Because there is no exchange to serve as a clearing house for OTC stock, the OTC broker must try to locate the stock and buy it at a profitable price. He may happen to have Magic Metal stock on hand in his own inventory. But if he doesn't, he will consult the daily report of the National Quotations Bureau. These reports provide the asking prices on thousands of unlisted stocks and name the dealers from whom they can be purchased.

Let us suppose the broker is able to buy Magic Metal for 101½, or $101.50 a share. He sells it to his customer for about $105 a share. The difference between the broker's buying and selling price is called mark-up. It is his profit, the pay he receives for his services. The National Association of Securities Dealers governs all OTC brokers, and sees that their mark-ups are fair ones.

For the average investor, dealing with OTC securities has several disadvantages. Buying or selling OTC stocks is a much slower and more complicated operation than trading stocks listed on an exchange. Also, the investor may find it difficult to keep informed about what his stocks are doing, for he can't always open his local newspaper and find the opening and closing prices of OTC stock. Only the most popular, or active, stocks are listed under OTC trades in the newspapers.

One of the most popular kinds of over-the-counter stocks is an investment trust called a mutual fund, or open-end trust. This is an investment fund managed by professional investment experts.

People buy shares in the fund itself. The fund takes the money collected from all of its shareholders and invests it for them in a wide variety of stocks. Each shareholder owns a certain percentage of the stocks bought by the fund, and each receives a certain percentage of the dividends and profit earned on that stock. In return, the shareholders pay the fund managers for their professional services.

There are approximately 200 mutual funds doing business in the country today. Their size is enormous, both in the number of shareholders involved

MUTUAL FUNDS

ADVANTAGES
- Professional Management
- Diversification
- Possible Higher Profits

DISADVANTAGE
- Fee Required by Management

and in the amount of money they have for investment. Several funds have hundreds of millions of dollars in stock holdings, and a few have over one billion dollars.

Mutual funds have become popular because they offer investors professional management of their money and diversification—that is, investment of their money in hundreds of different companies. Through a mutual fund, an investor can benefit from a far wider range of investments than he could afford himself. This often gives him higher profits and more security than he could get investing on his own. For this, of course, he must pay the mutual fund a rather large fee. The usual fee is 6 to 9 percent of his investment. This cost is considered by many people to be the disadvantage of mutual funds.

Another type of investment trust is the closed-end company. It operates in nearly the same way as the mutual fund. The chief difference is that the closed-end company is authorized to sell only a certain number of shares. When these are sold, the company is "closed." No new shareholders can buy into the company unless a current stockholder sells his stock. On the other hand, a mutual fund, or open-end company, is always open to new shareholders. It is continually offering more shares to the public.

SUPER WHEELS INC
PRESIDENT
STOCK CERTIFICATE

6
Owning Stock

Now let us return to the young investor who has just purchased stock in Super Wheels. A few days after placing his order, he and his parents receive a bill from their broker telling them exactly how much they must pay for the transaction.

The bill might look like this:

PRICE FOR ONE SHARE OF SUPER WHEELS	$19.75
10 SHARES OF SUPER WHEELS	$197.50
MINIMUM BROKERAGE COMMISSION	$6.00
TOTAL	$203.50

This is how the price for one share of Super Wheels was determined. The market price, which is the price agreed to by the broker on the floor of the exchange, was 19⅝, or $19.62½ a share. To this was added the odd-lot dealer's fee of 12½¢, or ⅛ of a point, making the total cost $19.75 a share. (Had the share been $40 or more, the odd-lot charge would have been 25¢ a share.)

The price of the 10 shares was determined, of course, by multiplying $19.75, the price of one share, by 10.

The money a broker charges an investor for acting as his agent is called a commission. All brokers' commissions are set by law. They are determined by multiplying the price of the stock transaction by a percent stated in the law.

The commission on the investor's purchase of Super Wheels was figured from the tables below, established by the New York Stock Exchange. Since the order was for 10 shares, the odd-lot table was used. As determined earlier, the price for all 10 shares was $197.50. In this price range, the table shows the broker's commission as 2 percent plus $1. Two percent of $197.50 is $3.95; to this is added $1, for a total of $4.95. Because this figure is less than $6, the least amount of commission permitted by law, the investor was charged the $6 minimum commission. Thus, his total bill equaled $203.50.

A few weeks after paying for his stock, the

MINIMUM COMMISSIONS

Round Lots

PRICE FOR EACH SHARE	COMMISSION
$1 to $4	Add $3 to 2 times the price per share
$4 to $24	Add $7 to the price per share
$24 to $50	Add $19 to ½ of the price per share
$50 and Over	Add $39 to 1/10 of the price per share

(*Never less than $6 nor more than $75 per 100 shares*)

Odd Lots

PRICE FOR ALL SHARES BOUGHT OR SOLD	COMMISSION
$100 to $400	2% plus $1
$400 to $2,400	1% plus $5
$2,400 to $4,999	½% plus $17
$5,000 and Over	1/10% plus $37

(*Never more than $1.50 times the number of shares. Minimum commission $6 and maximum commission $75. If the order is less than $100, the commission must be agreed upon by the broker and the customer.*)

investor will receive a stock certificate from Super Wheels, showing he is now a part owner of the company. The number of shares he owns will be typed on the face of this handsome paper.

The New York Stock Exchange Clearing Corporation, which is owned by the exchange, handles the stock certificates and payments that shift back and forth between buyers and sellers. The corporation receives stock certificates that have been sold and redistributes them to brokers whose customers have bought the stock. At the same time they transfer the money involved in these trades.

It is a very complicated transaction, and this is how it works.

When the clearing corporation sends an investor's stock certificate to his broker's New York office, the certificate is, of course, made out in someone else's name—the name of the person who just sold it. To have this changed, the brokerage firm sends the certificate to its transfer agent in New York. The agent is usually a bank or trust company, which cancels the old certificate and issues a new certificate in the new investor's name. A different bank then double-checks the certificate for accuracy, registers the investor as the new owner, and returns the certificate to the brokerage firm, which sends it on to the investor. All of this takes about two weeks or more.

To simplify this operation, stock exchange officials hope soon to replace stock certificates with standard-sized punch cards, each coded with an identification number.

A stock certificate is as valuable as money and should be treated just as carefully. When the in-

ROUTE OF STOCK TRANSFER AFTER SALE

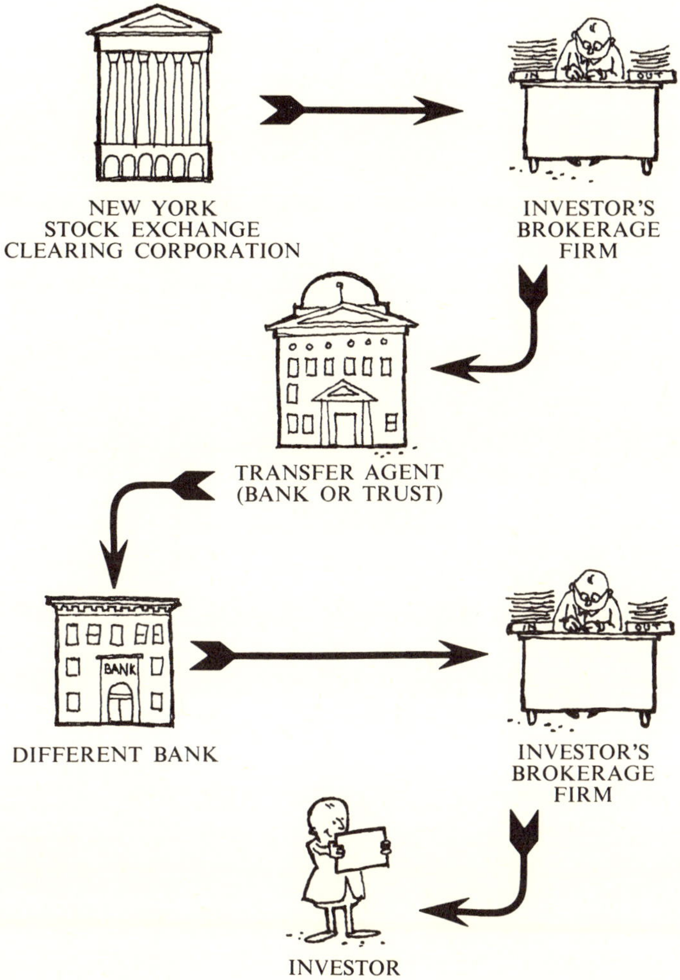

vestor receives his certificate, he should store it in a vault box or other safe place.

Although nearly 1½ million children now own stock, the law says that no one under 21 years of age may hold stock in his own name. Therefore, parents must buy stock for their child in their own names and must act as custodians of the shares until the child is 21. Then the young investor is allowed to take over the shares himself.

One of the privileges given to owners of common stock is the right to vote on company business. This right, however, is not given to stockholders under 21. Their parents vote in their place.

Stockholders' voting rights usually are exercised once a year at the company's annual open meeting. All stockholders are invited to attend this meeting to hear the company's annual report and to elect the board of directors for the coming year. Also, stockholders can question company officers about the firm's operation and can voice complaints if they are not satisfied with the way things are going.

If a stockholder cannot attend the meeting, which is the usual case, he can still vote by proxy. This means he mails back a slip giving another stockholder, usually a company director, the right to his vote.

Sometimes strange and funny things happen at annual meetings. A few years ago, at the annual meeting of a giant corporation, picnic lunches were served to all stockholders. When the time came for the stockholders to question company officers, one woman clamored for attention. When an officer finally called on her, she rose and asked, "What is the recipe for this delicious chicken salad?"

Funnies
FINANCIAL
SECTION

7
The Financial Pages

Once the beginning investor has become a stockholder of Super Wheels, he will want to keep track of his investment—to see whether his stock rises or falls in value. The easiest way to follow most stocks is by reading the financial pages of the daily newspaper. Although the small print looks uninviting and some of the symbols resemble a secret code, the financial pages can be fascinating and easily understood—if one takes the time to learn how to interpret them.

Most newspapers list both the New York Stock Exchange and the American Stock Exchange. Let us suppose Super Wheels is listed on the New York Exchange. It would be listed alphabetically and would take up one line. That line might look like this:

SuWls 1 61 21 19 20 +¼

Su Wls	1	61	21	19	20	+ 1/4
NAME OF STOCK	YEARLY DIVIDEND	UNITS OF 100 TRADED	DAY'S HIGH	DAY'S LOW	CLOSING PRICE	NET CHANGE IN LAST 24 HOURS

Su Wls is the abbreviated name of the stock. It is a common stock. If the letters pf. or pfd. appear after the stock name, it is a preferred stock. Companies that have both kinds of stock occupy two lines.

The number 1 means $1 and is the dividend paid on one share of Super Wheels for one year. If no figure appears here, the company does not pay a dividend.

The number 61 is the number of shares traded on this day in units of 100. This means that 6,100 shares were traded during this market day.

The number 21 stands for $21, the highest price a share sold for this day. The number 19, or $19, is the lowest price a share sold for. Sunday newspapers also give the highest and the lowest price the stock sold for during the year.

The number 20 is the closing price, the price paid for a share on the last sale of the day. Therefore, Super Wheels is now selling for about $20 a share.

The fraction +¼, or plus 25¢, means that the closing price, paid on the last sale of the day, is one-quarter point above yesterday's closing price. This is called the net change, and it shows whether the stock has gone up or down in price. If it has gone down, it is shown by a minus sign. If there has been no change, a series of dots is used. Remember, when the market reports speak of points, they mean dollars.

The market reports for bonds are read in nearly the same way as stock reports. The only difference is that bond prices are given in units of 1,000, shortened by dropping the last zero.

Reports on over-the-counter trades are also found in the financial pages. Unlike the stocks sold on the exchanges, only the most popular and active OTC stocks are listed in the newspapers, and less information is given about them. Each listing begins with the company's name. The latest price bid for the stock and the latest price asked are shown, and sometimes another column tells the last previous bid offered for the stock.

A familiar name found in the financial pages is Dow-Jones. Radio and television announcers often mention this name when they report stock market news. It stands for the Dow-Jones Stock Averages, which show whether the stock market is moving up or down.

A company founded in the 1880's by Charles H. Dow and Edward D. Jones figures the averages. They are figured in this way. Each day a record is

made of the closing prices of certain stocks in various fields. These prices are averaged and mathematically adjusted to take into account such things as stock splits and dividends. Then the average is compared with the average of the day before. If the new average is higher, the stock market is said to have gone up. If it is lower, the market has gone down. For example, if the average shows —1.25, the market is, on the average, $1.25 lower than the day before.

Averages, of course, are just indications of the *general* direction of the market. Individual stock prices may sometimes go in the opposite direction.

The stocks used in figuring the Dow-Jones Averages are not random choices. They are specially selected key stocks that are representative of their industry or field. For example, Chrysler Corporation and General Motors are key stocks in the automobile industry. The use of key stocks helps to make the averages representative of the whole stock market.

Fields covered by the Dow-Jones Averages are: Industrials (30 selected businesses); Rails (20 railroads); Utilities (15 gas or electric companies); and the Composite (all 65 stocks together). Only the industrials are used, however, to show if the market is up or down. Therefore, when the newscaster says, "The Dow-Jones Average is up three points," he means that the average price for the 30 stocks making up the Dow-Jones Industrials rose $3 over the day before.

Although the Dow-Jones is the most popular, there are other well-known market averages that many people follow. These include Standard and Poor's 500-Stock Index, the Associated Press Averages, and other averages figured and published by some major newspapers. Many people find these averages helpful in evaluating the current market situation and in predicting what will happen to stock prices in the future.

MISS
MARKET

8

What Makes the Market Move?

Much of the fascination of the stock market, for a beginning or a professional investor, is watching stock prices move up and down. But soon the beginner wonders *why* those prices move. Why is a share of a giant company like Commonwealth Edison worth more one day than the next?

The reason lies in the economic theory of supply and demand. There are only a certain number of Commonwealth Edison shares to be traded, so price depends upon whether more people want to buy shares than sell them. If more people want to buy shares on a certain day, the price will go up. If more want to sell that day, the price will go down. Stock prices are determined by the balance between the number of buyers and sellers.

Two rather strange words are used to describe stock buyers and sellers. They are "bull" and "bear." When the beginning investor decided to buy Super

Wheels, he became a bull because he believed the price of that stock was going up. A bull market, therefore, is one that is going up. The opposite, a market that is going down, is called a bear market, just as people who are selling their stock are known as bears.

It is the way people think that determines whether they are bulls or bears. Several things influence investors' thinking. Possibly the most important is the daily newspaper.

The news on the financial pages can be especially influential. If, for example, a company announces it made a bigger profit this year than last, many people tend to think it will continue to prosper. They invest in it, and the price of its stock often goes up.

News of national and world events can also affect the opinions of buyers and sellers. If investors think the election of a certain president will bring prosperity, they buy and prices rise. If they fear the effect of a labor dispute on a major industry, they sell and prices fall. It is not the event, but the way people interpret it, that determines stock prices.

In addition to newspapers, there are a great many publications that have an influence on investors. These include company reports, analyses from brokerage houses, and dozens of weekly newsletters that predict future market trends and give advice on buying, selling, or holding various stocks. Like most magazines, these newsletters are sold on a subscription basis.

All of the information received by an investor influences his thinking and helps to determine whether he will be a bull or a bear, a buyer or a seller. What he thinks, and what all other investors think, makes the stock market move.

Market experts use many methods to predict the future of certain stocks and the market as a whole. Perhaps the oldest formula used to select a stock for investment is the price-earnings ratio. It is figured by dividing the price of a share by the earnings per share. Earnings should not be confused with dividends. Earnings are the corporation's entire profits, which may or may not include dividends. The earnings per share of a certain stock may be found in the company's annual report and in various stock analyses available from any broker.

Let us figure the price-earnings ratio on a stock selling for $60 a share which, in its last fiscal year, earned $3 a share. The price, $60, divided by the earnings, $3, gives a P-E ratio of 20. The stock, in other words, is selling at 20 times its earnings.

WALL STREET JOURNAL
BUSINESS WEEKLY
Newspapers
ANNUAL REPORTS
CAUTION
TIPS
DANGER
PROSPECTUS

As explained earlier, the price of every stock represents an opinion of what that stock is worth. In the past many investors thought that stock selling for more than 10 times its earnings was overpriced. But, with the condition of the stock market today, people are willing to buy stocks at price-earnings ratios of 20, 30, and even more because many companies are growing so rapidly they soon bring the ratio back into line. The danger in buying stocks with very high P-E ratios, however, is that the growth which was eventually supposed to bring 10 times earnings may never occur.

The more an investor studies the stock market, the more he realizes how much there is to learn about it. There are many ways to buy and sell stock that are advanced and should not concern a beginner. Such techniques are for speculators, persons who take high risks when they buy stocks, hoping to make a quick profit. Although these techniques may never be used by the average investor, it is worthwhile knowing what they are.

For instance, "margin buying" is a phrase that has been in the news a great deal in recent months. Buying on margin means buying stock on credit. A certain percent of the total stock purchase is required as a down payment. The rest is borrowed from a brokerage firm. The Federal Reserve Board sets the percent required.

In June, 1968, the required down payment was raised to 80 percent of the purchase price in an effort to slow down this risky buying method. Although this rate is high, it still allows an investor who buys $3,000 worth of stock to pay only $2,400 for it, if he buys on margin. The rest of the money is borrowed from his brokerage firm. Of course, he must pay the firm interest on the $600 loan.

Margin buying allows an investor to buy more stock than he could buy with the money he has on hand. If the price of the stock goes up a great deal, as he hopes, he will be able to pay the interest on his margin loan and the broker's commission and still make a profit—more profit than he would have made if he had bought only the number of shares he had money for.

If he guesses wrong, however, and the price of the stock goes down, the New York Stock Exchange requires that one of two things be done. Either his broker must collect more money from him, or enough of his stock must be sold to bring the margin loan and the present value of the stock back into line.

Like margin buying, selling short is a risky

technique of the professional investor. It is the bears who sell short. They sell borrowed stock on the belief that the stock will go down in price and they will be able to replace it later at a lower price.

For instance, through his broker, an investor borrows 100 shares of World Wide Toys selling for $10 a share, and sells them for $1,000. World Wide's stock dips to $5 a share, and the investor is able to replace the 100 borrowed shares for $500. This leaves him a profit of $500 (less commissions) on his original $1,000 sale. If he guesses wrong and World Wide goes up to $15 a share, he will have to replace the borrowed stock for $1,500, thereby losing $500.

Limit and stop orders are other techniques used by experienced investors. In a limit order the investor tells his broker the exact price (or better) at which he wants to buy or sell a certain stock. In other words, he sets a limit. He also states how long he wants the order to remain in force—a day, a week, or until cancelled.

A stop order is used to protect a profit or to limit a loss. Suppose an investor bought Midwest Airlines at 20 and entered a stop order with his broker to "sell at 17." In this way, if he guessed wrong and the stock fell in price, his loss would be held down. But let us suppose Midwest soared from 20 to 43. To protect some of his profit, the investor might enter a stop order to "sell at 35." Then, if the stock fell to that price, his shares would be sold and he would still have a 15-point profit.

These are just a few of the advanced market

techniques used by investors with money, nerve, and skill. It would be foolish for any beginner to think that these methods lead straight to a pot of gold.

A beginning investor must realize that there will be times when stock prices will go up and

times when they will go down. No one knows for sure when it will happen or why—only that it always happens.

Many people think they are experts and try to predict the market's turns. If they are correct, they often have just guessed right. Even the real experts—people who work in the stock market and have studied it for years—cannot know the market's future for sure. The Dow-Jones Averages may help people to judge the market, but even it cannot predict whether stocks will go up or down.

There is an old story about a man, wise in the ways of the stock market, who claimed he could predict whether prices would rise or fall. When someone came to him for advice, this is what happened. He would tell the hopeful investor that the market was going up; then, after the person left, he would write "down" on a file card. Or he would say that the market was going down, and then write "up" on the card.

If his prediction was correct, the investor he had advised would declare, "What a genius!" If his prediction was wrong, he would tell the disappointed person that he must have misunderstood the prediction. As proof, he would pull out his file card—on which he had written the opposite word.

For many years now the United States has been prosperous. Stock prices have climbed as the country's business has grown and prospered. Each day new investors join the 25 million Americans who already own stock. Through their investments, these stockholders own a very real share of the nation and its future.

Index